A Pet's Life

Rabbits

Anita Ganeri

Heinemann
LIBRARY

www.heinemann.co.uk/library

Visit our website to find out more information about **Heinemann Library** books.

To order:

☎ Phone 44 (0) 1865 888066

📄 Send a fax to 44 (0) 1865 314091

💻 Visit the Heinemann Bookshop at www.heinemann.co.uk/library to browse our catalogue and order online.

First published in Great Britain by Heinemann Library, Halley Court, Jordan Hill, Oxford OX2 8EJ, part of Harcourt Education.
Heinemann is a registered trademark of Harcourt Education Ltd.

Editorial: Jilly Attwood and Claire Throp
Design: Richard Parker and Tinstar Design Limited (www.tinstar.co.uk)
Picture Research: Rosie Garai
Production: Séverine Ribierre

Originated by Dot Gradations
Printed and bound in China by South China Printing Company

ISBN 0 431 17760 0
07 06 05 04 03
10 9 8 7 6 5 4 3 2 1

British Library Cataloguing in Publication Data
Ganeri, Anita
   Rabbits – (A Pet's Life)
   636.9'322
A full catalogue record for this book is available from the British Library.

Acknowledgements
The publishers would like to thank the following for permission to reproduce photographs: Ardea **pp. 5**, **6** (John Daniels), **26** (Johan D. Meester); Mark Farrell **pp. 9, 12, 13, 16, 17, 20, 21**; RSPCA **pp. 4** (E. A. Janes); Tudor Photography **pp. 8, 14, 15, 18, 19, 24, 25, 27**; Warren Photographic **pp. 7, 10, 11, 22, 23** (Jane Burton)

Cover photograph reproduced with permission of Alamy/Martin Ruegner.

The publishers would like to thank Pippa Bush of the RSPCA for her assistance in the preparation of this book.

Every effort has been made to contact copyright holders of any material reproduced in this book. Any omissions will be rectified in subsequent printings if notice is given to the publishers.

Contents

Any words appearing in the text in bold, **like this**, are explained in the Glossary.

What is a rabbit?

Rabbits are very popular pets. They come in lots of colours, from black to golden brown. There are many different sizes of rabbits, from tiny to huge.

Small rabbits, like these Netherland Dwarfs, are good for beginners to keep.

Here you can see the different parts of a rabbit's body and what each part is used for.

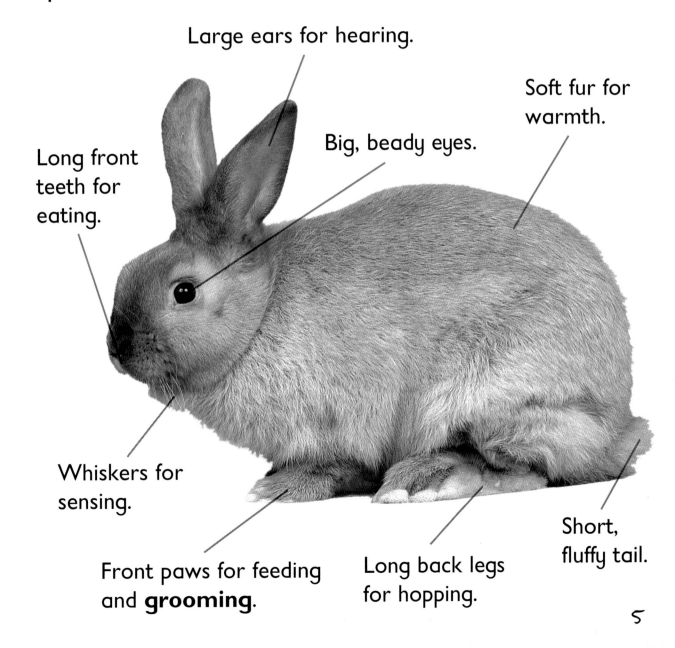

Large ears for hearing.

Soft fur for warmth.

Big, beady eyes.

Long front teeth for eating.

Whiskers for sensing.

Front paws for feeding and **grooming**.

Long back legs for hopping.

Short, fluffy tail.

Rabbit babies

Baby rabbits are called **kittens** or bunnies. They are born with no fur and with their eyes closed. A mother rabbit may have as many as eight babies in a **litter**.

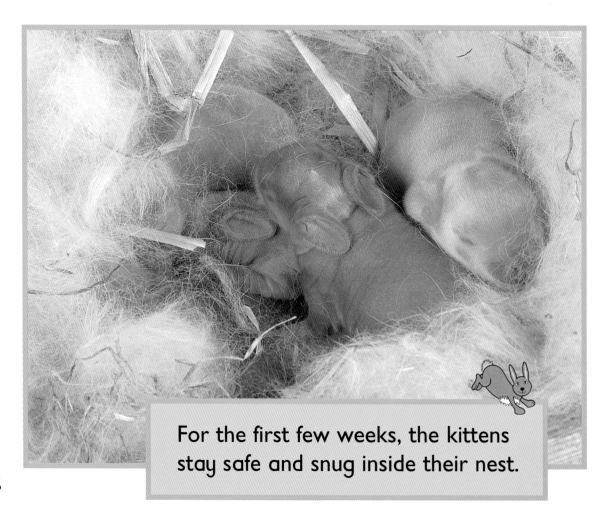

For the first few weeks, the kittens stay safe and snug inside their nest.

The kittens are old enough to leave their mother when they are about eight weeks old. Then they are ready to become pet rabbits. Don't disturb very young rabbits.

Rabbits can have lots of babies. It is best to keep males and females apart.

Your pet rabbits

Rabbits are fun to keep as pets but they need lots of care. You must be a good pet owner and learn to look after your rabbits properly.

Rabbits are very friendly and love to be stroked.

When you go away on holiday, ask a friend or neighbour to take care of your rabbits. Write a list of what your friend should do.

Your rabbits need fresh food and water every day.

Choosing your rabbits

Animal shelters are often looking for good homes for rabbits. You can also buy rabbits from good pet shops or from rabbit breeders.

Rabbits get lonely so keep two together. It is best to keep two female rabbits together.

Choose rabbits that look healthy and lively. They should have glossy coats, clear, bright eyes and clean teeth.

A rabbit with a runny nose may not be very well. This rabbit looks healthy.

Your rabbits' house

Your rabbits need a roomy house to live in. The rabbit house should have two rooms – one to live in and one for sleeping.

The living space has a **wire mesh** to let in light and air. The sleeping space has a solid door.

Line the bottom of the house with newspaper, covered with wood shavings. A good pile of shredded paper or hay makes a cosy bed.

Keep the house outside, raised off the ground.

Welcome home

You can take your rabbits home in a strong carrying box. Then leave them to explore their new home.

Make sure that the carrying box has air holes in it so that your rabbits can breathe.

Always pick up your rabbit properly. With one hand, gently grasp the scruff of its neck. Put your other arm around its bottom. Then lift it up.

Hold your rabbit close to your body to support its weight.

Playing with your rabbits

Rabbits need plenty of exercise. Make them an outside run in the garden with lots of room to hop about and **graze**.

Play with your rabbits every day. Otherwise they will get bored.

Put a strong **wire mesh** fence around the run. Make sure that it goes into the ground so that your rabbits cannot burrow their way underneath it.

The fence will keep your rabbits in, and dogs and cats out!

Feeding time

Pet shops sell special food pellets for rabbits. Rabbits need to eat plenty of hay. They also like to nibble on raw fruit and vegetables such as carrots and apples.

Rabbits also like cabbage, broccoli, turnips and dandelion leaves.

Feed your rabbits two small meals a day, in the morning and in the evening. Put the food in heavy bowls so that your rabbits can not tip them over.

Fix a **drip feeder** full of fresh drinking water to the front of your rabbits' house.

Cleaning the house

Rabbits are clean animals and do not like to live in a dirty house. Take away wet bedding and **droppings** every day to keep your rabbit house clean.

Once a week, sweep the house out.

Every few weeks, wash the house with warm, soapy water. Wash out the food bowls and water bottle every day. Always wash your hands after cleaning out your rabbits.

Give your rabbits fresh hay to sleep on.

Growing up

Some rabbits grow very big. When you choose a rabbit, find out how big it will grow. Large rabbits need more space than small or medium-sized rabbits.

You might need to get a bigger rabbit house as your rabbits grow up.

The sounds and movements your rabbits make are their way of talking. Rabbits stamp their back feet if they are cross or frightened.

Rabbits twitch their noses to smell other rabbits and tell if they are friends.

Healthy rabbits

You should check with a vet if your rabbits look unwell. A runny nose and eyes, or a dirty bottom may be signs of illness.

The vet will examine your rabbits for signs of illness or disease.

If your rabbits start scratching a lot, they might have fleas. Check their fur for tiny, dark specks, especially around their neck. These are flea droppings.

To control fleas, ask an adult to apply a 'spot-on' treatment from the vet.

Old age

If you look after your rabbits, they may live for up to six or eight years. As they get older, check them regularly to make sure that they are healthy.

Make sure that your rabbits get plenty of exercise so that they do not put on weight.

It can be very upsetting when your pets die. Try not to be too sad. Just remember the happy times you shared together.

Caring for your rabbits will help you learn how to treat animals properly.

Useful tips

- A rabbit's front teeth grow all the time. Give your pet a wooden block to **gnaw** on to stop their teeth getting too long.

- Your rabbits may need their claws clipping from time to time. A vet will do this for you.

- Rabbits **groom** themselves to keep their fur clean. But you need to brush long-haired rabbits, such as angoras, every day. You can brush short-haired rabbits once a week.

- You can keep two female rabbits together but it is best not to keep a rabbit with a guinea pig.

- If you keep a male and a female rabbit together, you need to have them **neutered** to stop them having babies.

Fact file

- Wild rabbits are small and brown. They live in large groups. Their homes are underground burrows, called warrens.

- Rabbits were first kept as pets about 400 years ago.

- There are about 100 different **breeds**, or kinds, of rabbits. The largest kind of pet rabbit is the Flemish giant. It is about the size of a small dog.

- Dwarf rabbits are the smallest kind. They can weigh less than a bag of sugar.

- Lop-eared rabbits have the longest ears. They can grow over 60 cm long, longer than your arm.

Glossary

animal shelters places where lost or unwanted animals are looked after and found new homes

breed a type or kind of an animal

drip feeder bottle that lets water slowly drip out. It is fixed to the rabbit's house.

droppings rabbits' poo

gnaw to chew and bite

graze to feed on grass

grooming gently brushing your rabbits' fur. Rabbits also groom themselves, using their rough tongues.

kittens baby rabbits

litter a group of baby rabbits

neutered when an animal has had an operation to stop it having any babies

wire mesh a sheet of wire with holes in it

More information

Books to read
Me and My Pet: Rabbit, Christine Morley and Carole Orbell (Two-Can Publishing, 1997)

My Pet: Rabbit, Honor Head (Belitha Press, 2000)

Websites
www.rspca.org.uk
   The website of The Royal Society for the Prevention of Cruelty to Animals in Britain.

www.pethealthcare.co.uk
   Information about caring for first pets.

www.petnet.com.au
   Information about being a good pet owner.

Index

Titles in the *A Pet's Life* series include:

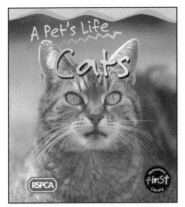

Hardback   0 431 17762 7

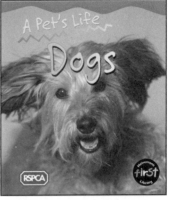

Hardback   0 431 17764 3

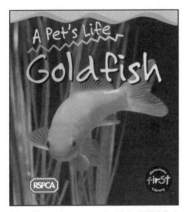

Hardback   0 431 17765 1

Hardback   0 431 17761 9

Hardback   0 431 17763 5

Hardback   0 431 17760 0

Find out about the other titles in this series on our website www.heinemann.co.uk/library